MW00638799

sweat

Success With Empathy and Trust

"Kivel provides space for coaches to reflect and grow as they're reading. The principles brought out in SWEAT can be applied beyond the realm of coaching — any reader can apply them to make a more prosperous future for themselves while uplifting everyone around them."

—Gillian Brassil, Former USA Artistic Swimming National Team Athlete, Sports Writer

"A coach's capacity (and willingness) to communicate can be quite varied, as well as complicated by the current circumstances. The specific communication strategies (verbal and body language), as well as journaling opportunities will definitely drive better results for Coaches who implement the SWEAT Playbook. "

—Jarmal Richard, High Performance Coach, Ultra Runner, Founder of iconnect2u Sports

"Emotional Intelligence empowers the coach to mentor athletes as mental and physical whole-human beings, to respond with positivity to the challenges that arise in training, competition and in life."

—Betsy Wells, 10-year member of the USA Freestyle Ski Team, World Cup competitor, 5x USA National Champion

"There are very clear and practical applications to the learning in SWEAT. Any coach, leader or athlete can pick up the book, read it and get better at what they do."

—Adam Andrasko, Chief Executive Officer, USA Artistic Swimming

"SWEAT is educational but also a very practical resource for coaches who want to inspire and motivate their athletes to grow and thrive within their sport but also beyond, in other domains of life. While the book was developed for coaches working with female athletes, I would recommend every coach read and use it!

—Christina W. Baker, Ph.D., Sports Psychologist, Rower

sweat

Success With Empathy and Trust

AN EMOTIONAL INTELLIGENCE PLAYBOOK
FOR COACHES OF FEMALE ATHLETES

SARAH KIVEL

www.sarahkivel.com
Published in Alamo, California

Library of Congress Control Number: 2021915584

ISBN: 978-0-578-96316-7 (hardcover)
ISBN: 978-0-578-96983-1 (paperback)
ISBN: 978-0-578-96418-8 (ebook)

Printed in China
2 4 6 8 10 9 7 5 3 1

First Edition

GRATITUDES

My deepest gratitude goes to ...

- All the coaches and athletes who have shared their time, hearts, stories, and experiences

- TJ, for your love, laughs, and never-waivering belief in me

- My mother, Katarina, who encouraged and coached me as an athlete throughout my life

- Tanner, Morgan, and Ryan for giving it your all

- Aiden and Liam, for your acceptance

- Team eiFOCUS™: Belinda, Betsy, Cherish, Cynthia, Jazmine, Patty, and Stephanie for your passion, enthusiasm, and commitment to girls in sports

- Mo, Tammy, and Janet for your dedication, inspiration, and passion for your sport and your athletes

- Coaches Bruce Renati and Greg Barber, who taught me what it felt like to be treated as a whole person and not just an athlete

- Editors Belinda H.Y. Chiu, Ed.D. and Ruby Peru, and book designer Eve DeGrie. I never would have finished without you!

AUTHOR'S NOTE

I will never forget my last soccer game as a collegiate athlete ... we were the home team, playing on one of the university campus fields. There was a small group of fans watching. My next memory of that day is turning in my jersey to the athletic department. It was my sophomore year. After ten years playing soccer, I quit. Just like that, it was over. To this day, I can still feel the emptiness, sadness, and disappointment inside.

This was the first time I can remember quitting anything in my life. It was also the first time I had a coach with whom I could not connect. I did not know how to tell her I was feeling stressed managing the twin demands of school and sports. I did not know how to share with her I was losing my drive and passion for the sport that had always been at the center of my life. She did not have the tools to talk to me, either. She never reached out to ask what was wrong. In fact, I am not sure she even noticed. I will never forget the last words I heard from the sidelines: "You don't even care." That couldn't have been further from the truth.

In my mind, I had two options: stay or go. I chose to go. Looking back, I wish that both my coach and I had the emotional intelligence skills that could have helped us have meaningful conversations to address the situation. Perhaps I would have decided to keep playing. I will never know for sure. But I do know this: the athlete-coach relationship is critical to the success of an athlete.

Over the past several years, I have had the honor of working with athletes and their coaches on building the skills of emotional intelligence and focus. While names have been omitted, and, in some cases, the sport changed for the sake of confidentiality, all the stories in SWEAT are based on real experiences, most at the elite level.

SWEAT is based on the intersection of my life experiences as an athlete, coach to athletes, and parent to athletes combined with my professional experience as an emotional intelligence executive coach and consultant.

As coaches, we can teach technical skills, no problem. Sometimes, though, it's not so easy to know what to do when we notice a stressed, demotivated, or sad athlete. My hope is that SWEAT will give coaches the tools to empower themselves and their athletes to thrive in both their sports and lives.

Looking back, I wish that both my coach and I had the emotional intelligence skills that could have helped us have meaningful conversations to address the situation. Perhaps I would have decided to keep playing.

TABLE OF CONTENTS

A VISUAL REPRESENTATION OF EMOTIONAL INTELLIGENCE 10

COACHING FOR A NEW KIND OF WIN 12

THE IMPACT OF GREAT COACHING ON GIRLS 14

WHY EMOTIONALLY INTELLIGENT COACHING

WORKS BEST FOR GIRLS 16

HOW TO USE THIS BOOK 17

WHAT IS EMOTIONAL INTELLIGENCE? 17

INNER AND OUTER WORK 18

The Research 20

First (and Always) Do the Inner Work 20

PART 1: eiBoosters 24

eiBooster #1: Sleep 26

eiBooster #2: Gratitude 27

eiBooster #3: Focus 28

eiBooster #4: Movement 30

eiBooster #5: Awe 31

PART 2: THE ELEMENTS OF EMOTIONAL INTELLIGENCE 34

ELEMENT #1: Self-Awareness 36

ELEMENT #2: Emotional Control 44

ELEMENT #3: Agility 52

ELEMENT #4: Drive 60

ELEMENT #5: Positivity 68

PART 3: ATHLETE AWARENESS AND TEAM LEADERSHIP SKILLS 76

ELEMENT #6: Empathy 78

ELEMENT #7: Team Awareness 86

ELEMENT #8: Impact 94

ELEMENT #9: Friction Management 102

ELEMENT #10: Guide 110

ELEMENT #11: Teamwork 118

ELEMENT #12: Inspirational Coach 126

CONCLUSION 134

WORKS CITED 136

RECOMMENDED RESOURCES FOR A DEEPER DIVE 140

ABOUT THE AUTHOR 142

A VISUAL REPRESENTATION OF EMOTIONAL INTELLIGENCE

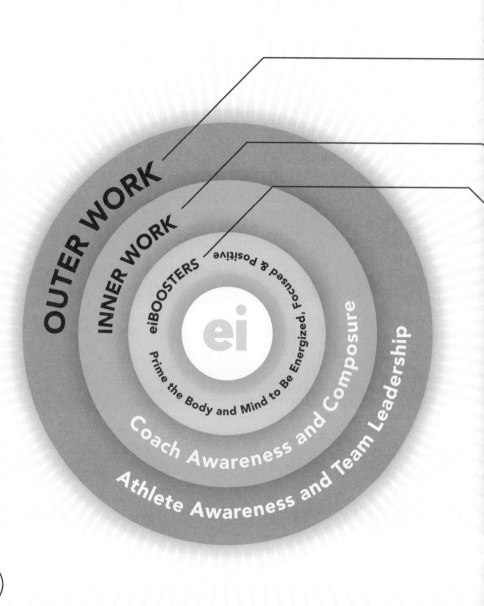

OUTER WORK

INNER WORK

eiBOOSTERS

Focused & Positive

Prime the Body and Mind to Be Energized,

ei

Coach Awareness and Composure

Athlete Awareness and Team Leadership

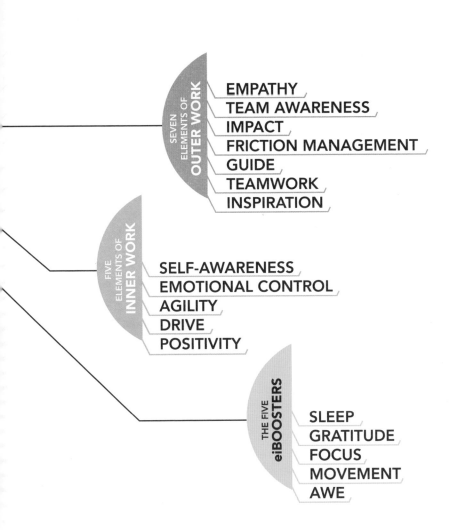

SEVEN ELEMENTS OF **OUTER WORK**
- EMPATHY
- TEAM AWARENESS
- IMPACT
- FRICTION MANAGEMENT
- GUIDE
- TEAMWORK
- INSPIRATION

FIVE ELEMENTS OF **INNER WORK**
- SELF-AWARENESS
- EMOTIONAL CONTROL
- AGILITY
- DRIVE
- POSITIVITY

THE FIVE **eiBOOSTERS**
- SLEEP
- GRATITUDE
- FOCUS
- MOVEMENT
- AWE

COACHING FOR A NEW KIND OF WIN

As coaches, we want to help our athletes perform at the top of their game. Quite literally, their success is our success. But nurturing the best performance can be a complex process. After all, the human brain doesn't always respond the same way to the same stimulus, and words that may encourage one athlete may discourage another, depending upon her personality and mood. Many coaches depend upon tried-and-true stock phrases and exercises (like "stay focused!" and "suck it up!") to boost athlete performance and morale, with mixed results. But research shows that if, instead, coaches use the principles of emotional intelligence, they can achieve far superior results.

emotional

Outside the limited world of social science and psychology, the term "emotional intelligence" is not as widely known as it should be, but that fact is rapidly changing. The past decades have given us evidence-based research in this field that definitively demonstrates how emotional intelligence leadership skills can be applied to improve athlete attitude, drive, and performance. It's time for coaches to take advantage of what top scientists know about how the human brain works. In so doing, we as coaches can learn the skills that will inspire and motivate our athletes to perform and succeed — not just on the playing field, but also in life. This is what great coaching is all about.

intelligence

THE IMPACT OF GREAT COACHING ON GIRLS

Like any great teacher, you, as coach, have the potential to permanently impact a young girl's life for the better. To achieve this, you must help girls believe in themselves, push past previous limits, work together, and exhibit leadership skills. While the principles of emotional intelligence can (and should) be used in myriad contexts, including coaching boys, girls respond especially well to coaches with a keen understanding of these principles. So, coaching girls, specifically, is the focus of this book.

Statistics show that there are enormous benefits for girls who play sports.

For instance:
- Girls who played sports have higher confidence levels at all ages.[i]
- Girls who play sports have higher GPAs and lower rates of depression.[ii]
- During adolescence and young adulthood, girls who participate in sports are 20% less likely to get breast cancer later in life.[iii]
- Female athletes who play sports during high school have more positive body images than non-athletes.[iv]
- 94% of female executives played sports, with over half playing at the collegiate level.[v]

94%

Let's take a look at that last statistic one more time. Yes, verifiable studies show that the vast majority of female corporate executives played sports, and most did it all the way up through college. That means they developed a life-long love of sport. For some, a sports scholarship surely won them the chance at the higher education needed for success and improved socio-economic status. With this evidence at hand, it's indisputable: Good coaches win games, but *great* coaches train the future CEOs of their nations.

As a coach, you train world builders, decision makers, and masters of the universe. As more women hold these high-level roles, society gets closer to a state of gender equality. So, when you stop and think about the future you'd like to create, please understand the contribution you, as a coach, are making. The principles and leadership skills of emotional intelligence are key to this achievement.

In summation: Coaching is important, not just on a day-to-day level but in the big picture of the lives of girls and women. Ultimately, your role as a coach can help make our world a better place.

WHY EMOTIONALLY INTELLIGENT COACHING WORKS BEST FOR GIRLS

Sadly, girls today drop out of sports at a rate that is two to three times higher than that of boys. The benefits of girls' sports are clear and proven, so it is incumbent upon coaches to prioritize player retention. The most successful coaches in this regard understand that girls need to be coached in a different way than boys.[vi] In the past, many coaches believed that girls' coaches should simply be less competitive. This is definitely not the case, nor do any studies support the notion that women or girls are less competitive than men or boys.

The fact of the matter is that coaching girls simply requires a different technique altogether. That technique is the subject of this book. You, as a coach, will find that not only does emotionally intelligent coaching make you a better coach for your athletes, but it will keep you in a more calm and positive state overall, especially when dealing with referees and others on the sports field who may trigger you, emotionally.

In order to be a successful coach to female athletes, it is important to understand how girls come to play sports in the first place and what keeps them playing. According to research from Nike and the Women's Sports Foundation, one of the main reasons that girls begin playing sports is to make and be with friends. In other words, their relationships with their teammates and coaches matter a lot. Within these relationships, girls want to be treated as whole people and not just athletes.[vii] While relationship-building might not traditionally be the focus of coaching, it is an essential element to coaching girls and is therefore the focus of this book. The secret to success lies in the principles of emotional intelligence.

As a coach, you teach critical leadership skills and help build inspiring relationships. By training with and embodying the leadership skills found in the principles of emotional intelligence, you will become the supportive role model that your athletes want and need. In turn, your athletes will keep playing long after they have left your team. With your help, they'll receive all the lifelong benefits of sports, including the personality traits that make them future leaders.

In our SWEAT training model, we have adapted the evidence-based leadership skills of emotional intelligence (which include mindfulness and gratitude) to athletics. Our training guides you through real-time, applicable exercises so that you can start training and building these new skills.

HOW TO USE THIS BOOK

SWEAT offers bite-sized learnings and practices that you can implement right away. This playbook is designed to be something you can throw into your gear bag and bring to practice and competitions. You can incorporate the trainings with your team, practice them on your own, and use them when conferencing with players.

WHAT IS EMOTIONAL INTELLIGENCE?

Emotional intelligence is the ability to recognize how you are feeling and understand how your emotions affect your performance and your relationships. Emotional Intelligence is not a new concept, nor is it rocket science. While elusive to many, those who learn its principles have a powerful coaching tool. Some believe emotional intelligence is akin to being a "sensitive person" or having a "nurturing personality," but this is misleading and a gross oversimplification. The fact of the matter is, all coaches can learn these skills, no matter what personalities they bring to the table.

17

INNER AND OUTER WORK

To teach you how to coach from the standpoint of emotional intelligence, we will address two facets of this work. First, we emphasize the inner work that enables coaches to heighten their emotional awareness and maintain their composure under stress. In this section, we discuss the skills that help you understand what you're feeling and how emotions affect your behavior. Next, we'll address the outer work or the skills necessary for understanding what others are feeling and how to use that knowledge for effective team leadership.

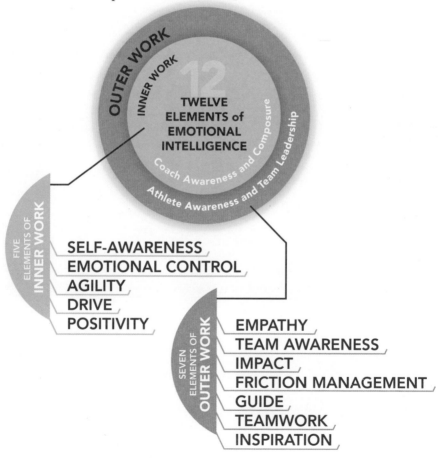

OUTER WORK
INNER WORK

12

TWELVE ELEMENTS of EMOTIONAL INTELLIGENCE

Coach Awareness and Composure

Athlete Awareness and Team Leadership

FIVE ELEMENTS OF INNER WORK

SELF-AWARENESS
EMOTIONAL CONTROL
AGILITY
DRIVE
POSITIVITY

SEVEN ELEMENTS OF OUTER WORK

EMPATHY
TEAM AWARENESS
IMPACT
FRICTION MANAGEMENT
GUIDE
TEAMWORK
INSPIRATION

THE FIVE ELEMENTS OF THAT INNER WORK INCLUDE:

- **SELF-AWARENESS**
- **EMOTIONAL CONTROL**
- **AGILITY**
- **DRIVE**
- **POSITIVITY**

Going forward, we'll talk about how to build up each of these elements in yourself.

Having grounded yourself in the inner work of emotional intelligence, you will then go on to utilize the elements of the outer work to coach and interact with others.

THESE SEVEN ELEMENTS OF OUTER WORK INCLUDE:

- **EMPATHY**
- **TEAM AWARENESS**
- **IMPACT**
- **FRICTION MANAGEMENT**
- **GUIDE**
- **TEAMWORK**
- **INSPIRATION**

Before going into more detail about these elements, however, it's important to understand the research behind emotional intelligence (or "ei") as a skill that is critical for success.

THE RESEARCH

Our framework for building emotional intelligence is based on the work of Dr Daniel Goleman. In the 1990s, Dr. Daniel Goleman first introduced emotional intelligence as being a key ingredient to success in his book, *Emotional Intelligence: Why It Can Matter More than IQ.*[viii] In later years, Dr. Daniel Goleman and Richard Boyatzis investigated and researched hundreds of leaders in organizations and found that while they all had some level of technical abilities, education, and intelligence, there was a subgroup known as "peak performers." Goleman and Boyatzis wanted to know: What was it about these exceptional leaders that made them so inspiring and motivating? Why did everyone seem to want to work for them? What made them so special and effective? What the researchers found was that emotional intelligence was the one trait that separated the peak performers from everyone else. The twelve elements mentioned in this book are adapted from Dr. Goleman's twelve "competencies of emotional intelligence."[ix]

In addition, building upon the work of Goleman and Boyatzis, the World Economic Forum[x] has stated that not only do organizational leaders and their teams benefit from "ei," but emotional intelligence is one of the top five skills needed for success in the 21st Century, overall.

FIRST (AND ALWAYS) DO THE INNER WORK

In Part 1, you will be introduced to eiBoosters, which are essential aspects of your inner work on emotional intelligence. These eiBoosters are lifestyle choices that help you be at your emotional best so that you can be there for your players.

Just as consistent strength training and aerobic conditioning are key for athletic fitness, consistent training with eiBoosters is key for emotional intelligence fitness. We encourage you to incorporate these eiBoosters into your everyday trainings and routines in order to take the twelve elements of emotional intelligence to another level.

In this book, each eiBooster is broken down into two parts:

1) information about why the Booster is important
2) tools to put it into action

Along with the eiBoosters, Part 2 will introduce you to the second aspect of the preliminary inner work needed for great coaching, which includes the "elements of emotional intelligence." Our main focus in this section will be to focus on the essential skills of coach awareness and composure.

Once you have begun your inner work as a coach, only then can you apply what you've learned to coaching others. With this in mind, Part 3 reveals the seven techniques to nurture athlete awareness and team leadership.

To make it as easy as possible to remember and apply these skills in the field and on the go, each element is broken down into five parts:

1) SKILL
2) STATS
3) GAME FILM
4) SPRINTS
5) PRACTICE NOTES

The **SKILL** section provides information on the particular emotional intelligence element in question, which you can apply right away.

The **STATS** section demonstrates how each skill is evidence-based and backed up by hard science.

The **GAME FILM** section provides sports-specific examples as to how each emotional intelligence skill has been shown to help (or the lack of it to hinder) performance and relationships.

The **SPRINTS** section provides short exercises for practicing and mastering your new emotional intelligence skill, many of which can be done right there in the field, as needed in the moment.

The **PRACTICE NOTES** section prompts you, as a coach, to reflect on your thoughts and experiences as you put each new skill into action. Research shows that journaling helps individuals understand their own feelings as they strive. They can therefore achieve goals more readily.[xi] Such reflection is an essential component of making emotional intelligence an intuitive aspect of how you coach every day. Each Notes section has one prompt to get you started.

A good coach makes you feel like you can fully trust them with what they're saying. They allow you to be people on top of being an athlete. They gain your trust and respect, which allows you to fully take in what they're trying to teach you. A good coach also creates a team atmosphere. They don't favorite any one person. Instead, they look at everyone as a valuable team player ...and they mean it when they say it.

-MORGAN, WATER POLO PLAYER

PART 1

THE FIVE eiBOOSTERS

SLEEP

GRATITUDE

FOCUS

MOVEMENT

AWE

eiBoosters

There are five eiBoosters: Sleep, Gratitude, Focus, Movement, and Awe. These aspects of any emotionally healthy lifestyle set you up for learning the skills of emotional intelligence by priming your body and mind to feel more energized, focused, and positive.

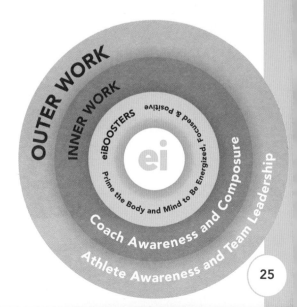

eiBooster #1: SLEEP

Sleep not only makes us feel good, but it also improves our performance in sports and all parts of our life. In order to receive the most benefit from sleep, we need eight hours of sleep (not five, six, or seven!). In fact, research proves that the last two hours of an eight-hour night of sleep provide 60-90% of your all-important dream state REM (rapid eye movement) phase. During these hours, sleep spindles, which are directly responsible for motor skill memory and its ability to turn training into performance, are hard at work. In addition, it is during this time that our brains get an "emotional tune up."[xii] Strengthening our own emotional intelligence with sleep is key to learning how to regulate our emotions and recognize the emotions of others.

PRACTICE

Exercise! But not within 2-3 hours of sleep. Exercise helps your brain and body relax, but working out too close to bedtime can be counter-productive. Your body temperature can remain high after exercise, making it difficult to drop your core temperature sufficiently to initiate sleep.

Allow yourself adequate time to prepare for bed. Reading, using dim lights or candles, and listening to soft music are soothing activities to prime yourself for rest.

Create a tidy, gadget-free bedroom environment that is conducive to sleep. Tidy up your bedroom and remove your gadgets so that distractions are minimized. Open the windows to cool down the room. (This is another way to drop body temperature to initiate sleep.)

eiBooster #2: GRATITUDE

Gratitude is a word for recognizing that there is goodness in our lives and that many of the benefits we enjoy are due to the actions of others. When we practice gratitude, we recognize the intention and effort that went into those actions on our behalf and the benefits they gave us.[xiii]

Gratitude is the practice of scanning your life and thinking about all the amazing people and things in it. Through this process, we train the brain to look for the good in all parts of our lives. When it comes to athletics, practicing gratitude has been associated with higher life, sport, and team satisfaction. Gratitude is also associated with higher levels of self-esteem and team cohesion. Furthermore, It is associated with better quality relationships with teammates and coaches as well as lower levels of athlete burnout and distress.[xiv]

PRACTICE

Gratitude Journal:
Write down 3-5 things you are grateful for at least once this week.

Three Good Things:
Write down 3 things that went well but also identify the causes of those good things.

Express Gratitude Directly to Someone:
This practice can be done by phone, letter, or face to face. (Research shows that this is the way to get the most well-being benefits from gratitude[xv])

eiBooster #3: FOCUS

You can think of focus training as strength training for the mind. We also refer to it as mindfulness. It strengthens the muscle of awareness and attention. The more we do it, the more attentive we become. After all, in order to build emotional intelligence to improve in our sport (or anything else, for that matter) we need to pay attention. With practice, focus training builds new pathways in the brain that help people become more aware, less stressed, more attentive, and less judgmental of themselves and others. It will also help you identify and manage your emotions.

Focus training is also known as "mindfulness." This is a way for coaches to learn to respond to both positive and distressing emotions in order to avoid reacting impulsively and thoughtlessly to the emotions. This training helps coaches prepare for competitions and practice in order to keep their attention on the athletes, not themselves.[xvi] Mindful coaches can better manage stress and keep their cool. Their athletes, in turn, benefit from having this important skill modeled for them.

As a coach, you know the importance of practicing a new skill over and over again before bringing it into a competitive arena, and the skill of staying focused is no different. For mindfulness training, or focus training, to have maximum benefit, it is critical to incorporate it into your daily routine, whether or not it feels necessary in the moment.[xvii]

PRACTICE

Below are a few simplified focus training exercises. The Greater Good Science Center (https://ggia.berkeley.edu) is a great resource to find the expanded version of each of these exercises. We encourage you to go to their website to explore the extended versions of these exercises. Experiment with each exercise and see which feels best for you. And remember, the more you practice, the stronger your focus and attention will become.

AWARENESS OF BREATH:

- Bring your attention to your breath.
- Notice how your body moves on the inhale and on the exhale.
- When your mind starts to wander off, notice this and bring your attention back to your breath.

MINDFUL MOVEMENT:

- On your next walk, pay very close attention to your feet.
- Notice how all the different parts of your foot hit the ground.
- Notice your speed.
- Notice what it feels like when you lift one foot and then the next.
- When your mind starts to wander off, notice this and bring your attention back to your feet.

MINDFUL EATING:

Before eating your next meal or snack, try practicing these mindful techniques:

- What does your food look like?
- Notice the different colors and textures.
- What does it smell like?
- Do you notice anything happening in your mouth or stomach?
- What does it feel like (if you can place it in your hand)?
- Place the food up to your lips and into your mouth.
- What does it feel like in your mouth?
- Begin to chew. What are the different tastes that arise?
- Swallow. What does it feel like when the food moves down your throat and into your stomach?

eiBooster #4: MOVEMENT

Many of us coach because we fell in love with our sport, and we want to share what we have learned with others. As life gets busy, though, many coaches stop playing and moving. Walking your talk is critical to being an influential leader. In particular, research shows that girls want and need role models. [xviii]

As a coach, you likely understand many of the health benefits associated with exercise and movement. Taking up a sport or fitness regime makes you feel in control of your body and your health. It also serves as a "time out" from a stressful day and can have positive effects for hours afterwards. When done with another person, it can also bolster social support and reinforce friendships.

In addition, movement is a key eiBooster for its emotional benefits. Exercise reduces anxiety and increases mood lifting hormones. [xix] When you can feel good physically AND emotionally, you create a strong foundation upon which to build your emotional intelligence. This takes effort and energy.

Movement can take the form of participating in a sport, such as the sport you coach, or maybe you'll want to try something new. Movement can also include activities like yoga, walking, biking, hiking, and so many other physical activities. Movement is simply moving your body.

PRACTICE

Maybe you already have an exercise routine that you love, or maybe you would like to try a mix of old and new movements or even get started once again with an activity you did long ago. Here are a few recommendations:

- Decide ahead of time on specific dates, times, and durations for your movement exercise.

- Choose a time of day, if possible, when you feel most energized.
- If you already engage in regular exercise, step it up. Run faster and longer, lift heavier weights, join a more advanced yoga class.
- Don't forget to rest, because as you know as a coach, recovery days are critical for peak performance.

eiBooster #5. AWE

Awe is a feeling of amazement that might "stop us in our tracks." It shifts our attention from ourselves, makes us feel like we are a part of something much greater than ourselves, and science even shows that it makes us feel more generous towards others.[xx]

Awe is the feeling we get when we see an extraordinary sunset or mountain range. We might feel awe when we listen to a beautiful piece of music, see an incredible work of art, or even watch a stellar athlete in action.

Awe can improve your mood and reduce stress. It can also increase feelings of connectedness, increase critical thinking, and get you into a positive mood.[xxi] In addition, awe helps us process information in a way that is less influenced by our expectations and more open to information that is actually real.[xxii] All of these qualities are essential to being a great coach and supporting you as you build your emotional intelligence. Awe also makes us feel more empathy,[xxiii] which is one of the elements of emotional intelligence.

PRACTICE

The world is filled with ways to inspire awe. Here are just some of them:

- Take a walk in nature.
- Read a story or biography about someone that you admire.

- Write about a time you experienced awe.
- Listen to a new genre of music.
- Look at pictures of beautiful places.
- Novelty is one of the keys to having awe-inspiring experiences, so mix it up and try something new.

As you begin to learn the skills of emotional intelligence, make these eiBoosters a part of your everyday training. You can think of them as the strength and conditioning workouts you need in order to develop the skills of emotional intelligence. They keep you strong and focused as you develop your new emotional skills and put them into play.

A good coach **motivates** *their athletes by making them* **want to be better.** *They lead by* **example** *and* **show** *their athletes that they* **care** *about them as a* **whole person.**

-RYAN, ARTISTIC SWIMMING ATHLETE

PART 2

FIVE
ELEMENTS OF
INNER WORK

SELF-AWARENESS
EMOTIONAL CONTROL
AGILITY
DRIVE
POSITIVITY

THE ELEMENTS OF EMOTIONAL INTELLIGENCE

Along with the eiBoosters listed above, the following five elements are the keys to building up your own self-awareness, which will, in turn, help you to better perceive the emotions of others and therefore strive for improved emotional states for everyone on your team. The first two (Self-Awareness and Emotional Control) come into play the most often in any coach's journey to improved emotional intelligence.

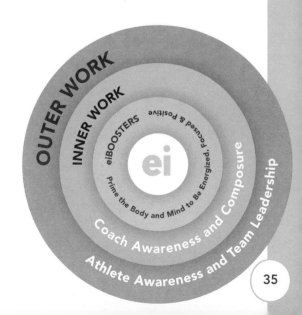

ELEMENT#1 SELF-AWARENESS

SKILL

It all starts here. When you can more accurately identify how you feel, you are less likely to get carried away by your emotions. Emotional awareness is the capacity to tune in to your own feelings, sense inner signals, and recognize how your feelings affect you and your performance. In fact, our emotions show up in our physical body before they register in your brain. If you can tune in to the clues your body is giving you and label your emotions, you've got the opportunity to influence what happens next. Emotional awareness is the foundation of emotional intelligence. When you know what's happening inside, you know how emotions affect your performance and relationships. This leads to a better understanding of how your emotions, in turn, affect you, your athlete, and her performance.

STATS

From *Beyond Emotional Intelligence: A Guide to Accessing Your Full Potential,* by S. Michele Nevarez:

"Our emotions are a particular expression of the way in which we perceive and try to make sense of our own sensory cues and signals."

GAME FILM

A water polo coach was easily distracted by a bad call from a referee. Not only did this increase her stress level, but it also took her attention away from her team. She took her stress out on her players, yelling at them and leaving them feeling quite demotivated. For the rest of the game, the team was left to continue competing on its own, without clear direction from the coach.

After starting her own emotional intelligence training, the coach was able to tune into what getting a bad call from the referee felt like in her body. Sometimes it felt like a tightness in her chest, and other times it felt like butterflies in her stomach. She became quicker to recognize these clues so she could take a moment to decide what to do next rather than unintentionally take her stress out on her players.

SPRINTS

A body scan helps us notice the different sensations in the body. It also helps us to better understand the clues our bodies give us. Wherever you are, pause for a moment. Bring your attention to the top of your head. Slowly work your way down your body to your toes. Notice the different sensations in your body. Use words that describe how the different parts of your body are feeling, like "tight," "relaxed," etc. Don't get stuck in one spot. Notice what it feels like, name it, and move on.

Repeat multiple times throughout your day.

PRACTICE NOTES:

What was it like for you to practice the body scan? Where did you notice your emotions showing up?

PRACTICE NOTES:

PRACTICE NOTES:

PRACTICE NOTES:

PRACTICE NOTES:

My favorite coach was one that made me **excited to show up at practice** *day in and day out. Having him as a coach* **made practices fun,** *yet I was* **still pushed to my limit** *every single practice. He was also someone who* **always believed in me** *and my abilities,* **even** *when I did not believe in myself. He made me truly love my sport.*

-ALICIA, DIVER

ELEMENT#2: EMOTIONAL CONTROL

SKILL

Keeping your cool under stress is key for peak performance and strong relationships. The moment one of your athletes makes a mistake, you may experience an emotion of anger or frustration. Being aware of the emotion, however, is not permission to express it freely. Managing your emotions and keeping your balance without being carried away is essential to good leadership.

Your immediate reaction can help or hinder your athlete's performance, team unity, and the competition's outcome. While a coach with very little emotional control might lose her cool, pull the athlete out of competition, and bench her, one with more self-awareness and emotional control will get better results by simply acknowledging the error while offering constructive feedback and coaching.

STATS

From *Mindful Sports Performance Enhancement* by Keith A. Kaufman, Carol R. Glass, Timothy R. Pineau:

"...although increasing optimism or decreasing anxiety may have utility, it is not the calibrating up or down of specific emotions but rather the capacity to respond adaptively to any emotion ... that may be the most beneficial..."[xxiv]

GAME FILM

When a basketball player made a mistake, the coach threw his hands up in frustration. When his athlete came to the sidelines, the coach said, "Your shot was awful! Haven't you learned anything at practice?" The impact of this reaction on the athlete was devastating. She was afraid to go back out on the court for fear of making another mistake.

Over time, the coach learned to acknowledge what happened in such moments without judging the incident itself. The next time his player missed a free throw, the coach said to himself, "The ball didn't go into the basket." That's it. He didn't react in frustration but, instead, followed up with a conversation about the specific play. This way, the coach could explain what the athlete might do next time without using language that "judged" her performance as an athlete.

SPRINTS

In the midst of an emotional moment, pause to notice what just happened without judging what happened. When you can take a moment or two before reacting to a mistake by one of your athletes, you are less likely to be carried away by your emotions and more likely to be able to stay present and focused on coaching. By managing your emotions, you model behavior that inspires your athlete to do the same. This will help her stay motivated and mentally in the game.

PRACTICE NOTES:

What does it feel like for you to slow down and pause in the midst of an emotional situation? What are the clues that a pause might be necessary?

PRACTICE NOTES:

PRACTICE NOTES:

PRACTICE NOTES:

PRACTICE NOTES:

A great coach allows me to be my real self. I know I can have fun while still being respected as an athlete and person. I can come to them with any problem, in or out of the pool, and I can always trust them. They make me feel confident in my abilities and they make me want to work really hard, while still enjoying myself.

-ANNA, SWIMMER

ELEMENT#3: AGILITY

SKILL

Emotional agility means adjusting to a new reality when things don't go your way. Sometimes it's also called "going with the flow." Agility helps us remain open to new ideas and different ways of doing things. It's our ability to be present and move with whatever is happening in the moment. Change is inevitable in sports and provides us with the thrill of not knowing what will happen next. The reality of constant change makes competition both stressful and fun. Coaches who are adaptable are able to handle change effortlessly. They can perceive change in situations on the ground, then adapt their own ways of doing things based upon that new information.

As the leader of your team, adapting to change is essential. In the worst-case scenario, change can stop us in our tracks, cause a loss of confidence, and result in coaches not knowing what to do next. When we fear doing things differently, we are not being adaptable to change, but when we come up with revolutionary or out-of-the-box ideas tailored to our new reality, we are expressing emotional agility.

STATS

From The Institute of Coaching:

"Emotional agility is a process that enables us to navigate life's twists and turns with self-acceptance, clear-sightedness, and an open mind. The process isn't about ignoring difficult emotions and thoughts. It's about holding those emotions and thoughts loosely, facing them courageously and compassionately, and then moving past them to ignite change in our life." [xxv]

GAME FILM

One soccer coach heard from her athletes that they were incredibly fatigued after long weeks of training leading up to a competition. The coach was used to actually ramping up practice times and intensity right before competition, but after listening to the athletes, even though it wasn't in her original plan, she decided to shorten practice slightly in order to give the athletes a little more recovery time. As a result, the athletes not only felt rested and ready for competition, but they felt that their coach cared about both their performance and their wellbeing. They ended up winning gold.

SPRINTS

Get curious. Pay close attention to your own behavior and ask yourself:

- How do I handle change?
- How well do I balance multiple demands or adapt to new situations?
- How resilient am I?
- How quickly do I bounce back from a difficult situation or hardship?

PRACTICE NOTES

Name and write down the different emotions that come up for you when things don't go the way you expect. Where do you feel these emotions in your body (e.g., tight jaw, rapid heart rate)?

PRACTICE NOTES:

PRACTICE NOTES:

PRACTICE NOTES:

PRACTICE NOTES:

A great player-coach relationship is built on trust and communication. With this foundation in place, a good coach will empower a player to push herself to new heights, both physically and strategically, while continuing to prioritize her mental well-being on and off the court.

-EMILY, VOLLEYBALL PLAYER

ELEMENT #4: DRIVE

SKILL

Drive is the mindset of striving to meet or exceed a standard of excellence. It is evident when individuals embrace feedback on performance and continually seek ways to do things better. As a leader and a coach, having drive also means supporting the goals of your athletes.

Drive is key for winning in sports. In order to create connection, trust, and open communication, it's important to identify your goals as a coach, those of each athlete, and those of the team as a whole. Pairing drive with empathy (or understanding another person's viewpoint) is key to leading high-performing athletes and teams.

STATS

From *Psychological Bulletin:*

"Results from a review of laboratory and field studies on the effects of goal setting on performance show that in 90% of the studies, specific and challenging goals led to higher performance than easy goals, 'do your best' goals, or no goals ... Goal setting is most likely to improve task performance when the goals are specific and sufficiently challenging." [xxvi]

GAME FILM

One lacrosse coach was feeling like an outsider on her own team. The team as a whole was having a hard time coming together to work toward its goals. This coach felt disconnected from the athletes and realized she didn't really know much about her players outside of their sport.

She decided to meet with each of her players one-on-one, before the season started. She asked questions about their lives and goals, and this helped her get to know each player as an individual. One of her top performers now plays for one of the best teams in the world. This player told her coach that she never would have gotten there if it had not been for her coach's support.

SPRINTS

Find out from each one of your athletes what her goals are ... not just in her sport but in her life. Check in with her regularly. Ask questions and get curious.

PRACTICE NOTES:

What do you notice about your relationships with your athletes when you learn more about their goals?

_____

_____

_____

_____

_____

_____

_____

_____

_____

_____

_____

_____

_____

_____

_____

_____

_____

_____

_____

_____

_____

_____

_____

_____

_____

PRACTICE NOTES:

PRACTICE NOTES:

PRACTICE NOTES:

PRACTICE NOTES:

I love when **coaches take the time** *to get to know me* *so we can* **connect** *on a higher level.*

-SENIA, VOLLEYBALL PLAYER

ELEMENT #5: POSITIVITY

SKILL

Positive outlook means seeing the positive in people, situations, and events. It isn't about ignoring harsh or negative realities, but rather having a growth mindset. Positive outlook helps build resilience and reinforces the skill of emotional agility in that it allows leaders to stay focused despite challenges that arise.

Having a positive outlook, especially during challenging times, brings your team together by promoting resilience and motivation. Something called "mirror neurons" in our brains reflect the moods of others around us, which means that, as a leader in your sport and on your team, your emotions are contagious. For instance, when someone smiles, we often smile back without thinking about it. These neurons allow us to learn through imitation. When a coach has a positive outlook, there is a great chance the rest of the team will, too.[xxvii]

STATS

From The Association for Psychological Science:

"Optimism motivates us and leads us to take initiative. Optimists don't easily give up. This is likely one reason that optimists are successful across a variety of arenas: professional, academic, athletic, social, and even health."[xxviii]

GAME FILM

One coach would often pull a player from competition when that athlete made a mistake. She started to notice a lack of enthusiasm from the athletes and finally realized that often the athletes would not understand what they had done wrong and why they were being taken out. This lack of understanding brought the players down, emotionally, and hampered their motivation and drive.

When the coach embraced positivity, it enabled her to make an important change. When an athlete needed to be pulled from the game, she would first acknowledge the player's effort and then coach her on what she might do differently next time. Then, she put the player back in the game to give her another chance to try again.

SPRINTS

Celebrate the successes of your athletes, no matter how big or small. With each correction you give, try adding two compliments or celebrations. Focus in on what the athlete did well.

PRACTICE NOTES:

As the coach, how does your positive attitude affect the team?

PRACTICE NOTES:

PRACTICE NOTES:

PRACTICE NOTES:

PRACTICE NOTES:

A great coach is someone that pushes me through my limits, helps me grow and teaches me values to help make my dreams a reality. They motivate me by giving me a long-term goal and by celebrating every little step that helps me reach this goal.

-SIXTINE, ROWER

PART 3

SEVEN ELEMENTS OF OUTER WORK

EMPATHY
TEAM AWARENESS
IMPACT
FRICTION MANAGEMENT
GUIDE
TEAMWORK
INSPIRATION

ATHLETE AWARENESS AND TEAM LEADERSHIP SKILLS

By now, it's clear: in order to lead with emotional intelligence, great coaches need to integrate eiBoosters into their lives. Now that you have learned those eiBoosters, and now that you've learned the five skills that build the inner strength required to coach with a focus on emotional intelligence, we're ready to talk about the seven additional elements of emotional intelligence.

The five elements of emotional intelligence listed above contribute to the coach's own development as an emotionally intelligent individual. To these, we need add only seven more elements, and these are the aspects of emotional intelligence that enable coaches to do the outer work that promotes athletes' own emotional awareness, provides team leadership, and enables coaches to better handle interactions with others on the field, such as referees, parents, and administrators. Part 3, therefore, details those seven crucial and final elements of emotional intelligence.

ELEMENT #6: EMPATHY

SKILL

Teamwork and competitive play are at their best when players have the ability to understand others. Empathy is a key part of this. Empathy is the ability to sense the emotions and understand the perspectives of others. Psychologists Daniel Goleman and Paul Ekman have identified three types of empathy.

- Cognitive (the ability to intellectually understand what someone else is feeling)
- Emotional (the ability to feel what someone else is feeling)
- Empathic concern, also known as compassion (the ability to understand and feel for someone else and to be motivated to do something about it).[xxix]

Empathetic coaches are able to relate to the different personalities of their athletes while actively listening and communicating effectively.

STATS

From *The Institute of Coaching:*

"When building good habits, many people will experience negative thoughts and emotions and moments of perceived failure. Coaches who know when to show sympathy can help validate contenders' feelings and allow them to get back on track. Good coaches know when to encourage a moment of pause and when to push competitors forward through the pain, walking that fine line between sympathy and empathy."[xxx]

GAME FILM

In an interview, one athlete described how her coach would sometimes say to her at practice, "you don't care." In truth, sometimes this athlete has an off day, and while it might appear that she "doesn't care," this is the furthest thing from the truth. This particular athlete cares deeply about her sport, so these words from her coach make her feel unheard and not cared for. As a result, this athlete is unmotivated and talks about burn-out and quitting.

When her coach learned how her words were impacting this athlete, she tried something new. She practiced listening, instead. When she held her athlete meetings, she focused on allowing the athletes the majority of the talking time. In this way, she was able to learn more about their lives. As a result, this simple but very important practice created a sense of trust and team bonding.

SPRINTS

Whether one-on-one or in a team meeting, talk less and listen A LOT more. Allow for that "awkward silence" and notice where the conversation goes.

PRACTICE NOTES:

Stop and think: What might your athletes be feeling right now? What can you do to support them?

PRACTICE NOTES:

PRACTICE NOTES:

PRACTICE NOTES:

PRACTICE NOTES:

> *A great coach always has open ears and is willing to listen and learn from their players just as much as they want to teach them. They also are able to adapt their coaching style to different players in order to create a community where everyone feels heard and supported.*
>
> -MADISON, WATER POLO PLAYER

ELEMENT #7: TEAM AWARENESS

SKILL

Understanding the dynamics of your team leads to success. Team awareness is having the ability to identify key influencers, networks, and dynamics within an organization. It's your ability to understand how decisions are made and who makes them.

As the leader of your team, it is important to understand the strengths of each athlete and how each athlete contributes to the team's success. Similarly, it is important to note the strengths of those peripheral to the team such as parents, club administrators, and others. That's why any peak performing coach can tell you who the key influencers are on their teams: the go-getters, the glue, the ones who get it done when the clock is ticking down. They're not always the athletes who draw the most attention, the loudest one, or even the best player. These coaches listen and pay close attention to the other team leaders and supporters around them. They also know on whom to call when they need support for the team as a whole. Coaches who pay attention to the explicit and unwritten rules, as well as the implicit team dynamics, can use the strengths of a group to reach success.

STATS

From *The British Psychological Association:*

"The coach-athlete relationship is not an add-on to, or by-product of, the coaching process, nor is it based on the athlete's performance, age, or gender—instead it is the foundation of coaching. The coach and the athlete intentionally develop a relationship, which is characterized by a growing appreciation and respect for each other as individuals. Overall, the coach-athlete relationship is ... at the heart of achievement and the mastery of personal qualities such as leadership, determination, confidence, and self-reliance."[xxxi]

GAME FILM

A soccer team was planning a travel tournament. As the tournament date approached, the athletes were noticeably distracted and stressed at practice. The coach was confused as to what was happening with her athletes. She held a meeting with the team captain and learned the athletes were excited but also very nervous about competing at this high level for the first time.

The coach responded by calling one of her friends who happened to be the coach of one of the competing teams who was also going to be at the tournament. She arranged for a pre-tournament scrimmage with this team that included plenty of time to stop the clock for coaching.

As a result, her team of athletes went into the tournament feeling confident, strong, and ready.

SPRINTS

Sometimes as coaches we can feel overwhelmed by the multiple responsibilities that we hold as the team leader. Notice the other leaders, supporters, and athletes in your organization. What are their strengths and interests? Ask them to assist you with a project or role that might be challenging for you to take on yourself.

PRACTICE NOTES:

Ask yourself: Is there a way to gain a greater awareness of the dynamics or systems in play in your organization?

PRACTICE NOTES:

PRACTICE NOTES:

PRACTICE NOTES:

PRACTICE NOTES:

> "Someone *can tell you* they *care about you,* but *when* you can *feel it,* it's so much more *real...* my coach is *positive, funny,* and *cool.* He is someone our team enjoys being around...."

— TL, WATER POLO AND
LACROSSE PLAYER

ELEMENT #8: IMPACT

SKILL

Having a positive impact on your team means being able to get support from your athletes. Impact is based on understanding other people's perspectives and incorporating this insight to help move people toward their goals. Leaders who are impactful will also be able to get support from others and create a motivated team. They do this by "walking their talk." Showing your athletes that you have the same expectations for yourself as you have for them is motivating and inspiring and builds trust—all keys to leadership. When athletes trust their leader, they are likely to be less stressed, have more energy, work harder, and feel better about their lives overall.

STATS

From *International Journal of Sports Science and Coaching:*

"Although the athletes often placed their coaches on pedestals, they also saw them as human. The athletes described how their great coaches were not afraid to make mistakes, show faults, or admit that they did not have all the answers. 'They don't act like they are better than you or above you. [Instead they] come … to your level and act human.' The athletes felt that their coaches were particularly human when they expressed emotions.'"xxxii

GAME FILM

One high-level coach would consistently yell at her athletes at practice. This was how she was coached, and so it became her natural style of coaching, too. Her athletes felt worn out by the communication and unmotivated. They stopped listening and became un-coachable.

After several years and a lot of feedback, she recognized what was happening and that she wasn't "walking her talk" or, in other words, showing respect. In order to improve the communication, she slowly started to change her ways. Her athletes saw the effort and her desire to connect. With practice and time, the coach learned to model the respect for her athletes that she expected in return. As a result, the team became inspired and motivated to work hard, not only for themselves but also for their coach.

SPRINTS

In order to become more influential and create greater impact on your athletes, here are a few questions to consistently ask yourself:

- Do you follow through with your commitments and promises?
- Are you authentic and real in your conversations with your athletes?
- What are your values?
- What are the team's values?
- Are your thoughts, words and actions in line with these values?

As a coach, you expect your athletes to show respect and be focused when they are at practice. As the leader of the team, ask yourself: How are you showing up to practice and competition? Do you hold the same standards for yourself as you hold for your athletes?

PRACTICE NOTES

Write the answers to the previous questions in a journal. Ask your athletes for feedback.

PRACTICE NOTES:

PRACTICE NOTES:

PRACTICE NOTES:

PRACTICE NOTES:

My coach empowers me. She inspires me to push myself to my limits, just as she has done.

-RORY, SKIER AND LACROSSE PLAYER

ELEMENT #9: FRICTION MANAGEMENT

SKILL

People who work and play together don't always agree. Sometimes there is friction and conflict. Friction management means helping others through stressful situations and bringing disagreements out into the open. Leaders with this competency take the time to understand different perspectives and work towards finding common ground on which everyone can agree.

Managing friction well helps your athletes stay focused and motivated. High performing athletes and teams spend so much of their time together in structured training, they seldom have a chance to talk about how they are feeling and what is going on for them. Simply allowing space and time for the athletes to share how they are feeling with each other and with their coach can have an instant calming effect.

Relationship conflicts within a team can hurt performance. By taking the time to allow for team discussion, you are more likely to get conflicts out into the open and discuss them in a collaborative way, making a positive impact on the team and the team's performance.

STATS

From Association for Applied Sport Psychology:

"There are four principles to keep in mind when trying to resolve conflict:
Active Listening. Displaying a willingness to listen can help alleviate conflict ...
Non-verbal Communication ... Be open and consistent in your body language, helping to diffuse emotion ...
Using 'I' statements ... if the speaker takes responsibility for her/his statements, others will be less likely to simply react and put up a defense.
Avoid common communication obstacles [such as:] advising, diagnosing, discounting, lecturing, threatening [and] preaching.[xxiii]

GAME FILM

A synchronized swim team was losing motivation. The coaches were snapping at the athletes and athletes were becoming irritated with each other.

The coach decided to hold a meeting where the swimmers could share their thoughts and feelings. The coach took action and made some changes as a result. By acknowledging and validating the different emotions and situations that were coming up for the athletes, the coach was able to compassionately manage the conflicts that were bubbling up. The athletes felt heard, and they felt important. The team became, once again, motivated and positive.

SPRINTS

There are many stresses that athletes and coaches have outside of their sport: work, school, family, friends, etc. It can be very difficult to "check these stressors at the door" before practice and competition. Be the leader that builds compassionate competitors who can manage conflict. Carve out a time during practice each week or every other week to allow the athletes to have this valuable time to connect with you and each other. Start out by asking athletes to use one word to describe how they are feeling. It might feel awkward at first, but keep at it.

PRACTICE NOTES

How might I lean into conflict and help my team do so ... with curiosity?

PRACTICE NOTES:

PRACTICE NOTES:

PRACTICE NOTES:

PRACTICE NOTES:

"*A **great coach** is someone who can see **a bigger vision** for your **potential** than **you can** see for yourself, and—once they've SHOWN you that possibility—**holds you accountable** to **becoming** that **best version** of yourself you can be.*"

-KRISTA, FIGURE SKATER

ELEMENT #10: GUIDE

SKILL

Giving support to your team lifts everyone to the next level. Being a true guide to your athletes is about promoting learning and development in others by giving feedback and support. It is about supporting the performance AND growth of the athlete. Great coaches and mentors ask the right questions rather than giving advice or telling others what to do.

As an athletic coach, you have technical expertise, and you share this with your athletes so that they can improve performance. Another very important part of being a great coach is the ability to support your athlete's growth in her sport (and in her life).

Done well, coaching is also about supporting your athletes to find the answers themselves, rather than always telling them what to do. When an athlete can figure out the answer herself, she is more likely to make long-lasting change. She is also more likely to have increased self-confidence and improved performance.

STATS

From Psychology Today:

"Opposed to more traditional approaches to teaching where a coach, typically, provided all of the answers and simply instructed athletes where to go and what to do, a more humanistic and contemporary approach is to facilitate learning and development. Of course there are various ways to accomplish this and no method is going to work all of the time, however, it is important to consider the potential influence that asking an insightful question can have on the development of athletes."[xxxiv]

GAME FILM

One high-level team coach was lucky enough to have recruited one of the top athletes in the world to play for her team. This athlete was from another country. They had one of the most successful seasons ever, but the coach noticed this all-star athlete's spirits and motivation declining throughout the season. The athlete wasn't happy. This coach started spending time with this athlete, asking questions about her goals and dreams. As a result of these conversations, the athlete realized she missed playing for her home country and her own national team. She made the decision to return home.

Shortly after she was named MVP in a world championship game, the athlete reached out to her previous coach and told her that she never would have achieved those dreams if it weren't for her support. Of course, the coach missed this all-star athlete but felt incredibly satisfied that she had made such a difference in her life.

SPRINTS

Inspire your athletes with stories about your own path. Don't be afraid to share the challenges you have faced over time. When you discuss successes and challenges, ask questions like, "What have you learned or what skill have you developed because of this particular success or challenge?" Actively show interest in all parts of your athletes' lives.

PRACTICE NOTES:

At what moments can you do more coaching than teaching? Think back to your own favorite coaches. What were some of the qualities that made them your favorites?

PRACTICE NOTES:

PRACTICE NOTES:

PRACTICE NOTES:

PRACTICE NOTES:

*A **sense of humor** is **paramount** to a great coach. Coaches give an **individual** or **team motivation** without taking themselves too seriously. Inevitably, he/she/they have **very little control over your performance** other than to **give you guidance**, knowing what **motivates you**, and to **accept** the outcome of your race/ match with **dignity** and **good sportsmanship**.*

-WENDY, BASKETBALL, CROSS COUNTRY, TRACK, SOCCER

ELEMENT #11: TEAMWORK

SKILL

Working as a team is key to peak performance. Teamwork is the ability to work with others toward a shared goal, participate actively, and share responsibilities and rewards. It also means contributing to the capabilities of the team as a whole. Teamwork is based on trust between athletes and their coach.

Teamwork builds spirit, pride, and effectiveness. Being a part of a team means being a part of something bigger than oneself. It means working hard and taking care not only for the benefit of the individual athlete, but for the benefit of the entire team.

Teamwork also means developing and promoting an environment that supports creativity and different points of view. This allows the athletes to speak their minds without fear of being teased or told theirs was a "bad idea."

STATS

From Science Daily:

"Once you've gained as much as you can from bringing the right people together, you have to look for the next competitive advantage ... Whether it's in the workplace of the future on Earth or in deep space, understanding the relational predictors of team success is going to be very important.[xxxv]

GAME FILM

One swim coach noticed her athletes being irritated by a particularly "bossy" teammate. The situation created friction between the athletes at practice. The coach decided to hold a team meeting. She brought a large white board where she could write down notes and ideas from athletes. As a group, they were asked to describe the qualities of a good teammate. Each idea was shared on the board. Throughout the season, they would refer back to these notes so that all teammates, not just the one in question, might learn how to improve their skills. As a result, there was soon less friction and more teamwork within the entire team.

SPRINTS

Work with your athletes to agree on a description of what it means to be a good teammate. As a team, make a plan to help each athlete become a good teammate.

PRACTICE NOTES

What does it mean to be a good coach? How will you keep working on being a good coach?

PRACTICE NOTES:

PRACTICE NOTES:

PRACTICE NOTES:

PRACTICE NOTES:

"*My favorite coach is encouraging, hard core, kind, direct (cuts to the chase), cares about me and has a strong connection with me.*"

-ARRIAM, SWIMMER

ELEMENT #12: INSPIRATIONAL COACH

SKILL

Inspirational leaders have the ability to bring out the best in others. Often, they do this by articulating a shared purpose that motivates others. They show vulnerability and are not afraid to share their mistakes. They are able to make things happen while guiding their team toward a common goal, even during challenging times. They embody many of the elements of emotional intelligence that we have discussed.

Vulnerability is key to inspirational leadership. An inspiring coach keeps the athletes motivated and excited to play. She shares stories about her success and failures. This is how she develops trust with her athletes. An inspirational leader motivates and brings out the best in others. She shows up and treats others in a real and authentic way.

STATS

From *Dare to Lead* by Dr. Brené Brown:

"Being vulnerable is being courageous. It is the willingness to show up and be all in when you can't control the outcome."[xxxvi]

GAME FILM

In one water polo game, the home team was behind the entire game. In the middle of the last quarter, the game became tied. The coach on the visiting team started to "lose it" with his players. He was stressed and started yelling and snapping at his players. The visiting team ended up losing 13-10 after being ahead the entire game. The coach did not inspire his team in that final quarter. The athletes were deflated and uninspired. Ultimately, this cost them the game.

The coach reflected on what happened in that final quarter. He had lost his cool, and this affected his athletes so much that they lost the game. This was not the coach he wanted to be. He shared these feelings and words with his team and began to change his ways. As a result, the athletes stayed engaged and motivated and finished their season in third place, which was a huge accomplishment!

SPRINTS

Think of an experience or situation that was difficult for you. At your next team meeting, share this experience with your athletes. Let them know what made it difficult for you and what you learned from the experience.

PRACTICE NOTES

What do you notice about the conversations with your athletes once you practice being vulnerable?

PRACTICE NOTES:

PRACTICE NOTES:

PRACTICE NOTES:

PRACTICE NOTES:

A good coach **recognizes** *their mistakes and isn't afraid to be* **vulnerable** *and* **apologize** *for them.*

-MACKENZIE, LACROSSE AND
FIELD HOCKEY PLAYER

sweat

CONCLUSION

Coaches have many different training tools, but most traditional coaching systems push athletes hard while omitting the superpower tool of emotional intelligence. SWEAT is here to change all that.

As a coach, you have the honor and opportunity to shape a girl's life. It is not an easy job and might sometimes feel like an overwhelming responsibility. By embodying the leadership skills of emotional intelligence, you will become the role model that will guide these girls into becoming the future leaders of tomorrow. Above all, remember that you must first apply these principles to your own life and emotional state before you can effectively use them to help others.

SWEAT is by no means a comprehensive study of emotional intelligence. Rather, it was meant to give coaches a taste of how they can, with some simple changes in outlook, integrate these principles into their coaching techniques with great efficacy. Soon, you'll notice how small changes in behavior, speech, and attitude really do improve team play and player happiness as well as rack up the points on the scoreboard.

To continue your learning and take a deeper dive, we have included additional reading at the end of this book, as well as recommendations on emotional intelligence training programs.

As you work to prepare you own emotional readiness for coaching, consider the following: As a coach, you are the CEO of your team. Your athletes count on you for more than developing their technical skills. You are their leadership role model, mentor, and guide. Your emotions impact your team's performance and your athletes' lives, today. More importantly, though, great coaching has a lifelong impact that, statistics prove, helps to build the leaders of tomorrow.

WORKS CITED

i   Hinkelman, Lisa et al, "A Deeper Look: A Girls' Index Impact Report. Press Release," ROX: Ruling Our Experiences: The Girls' Index. Accessed May 11, 2021, https://rulingourexperiences.com/girls-and-sports

ii   Hinkelman "A Deeper Look."

iii   "The Who What, Where, When, and Sometimes Why," The Susan G. Komen Foundation, Accessed May 11, 2021, https://ww5.komen.org/BreastCancer/LackofExercise.html?afId=1098#:~:text=Women%20who%20get%20regular%20exercise,percent%20%5B119%2D125%5D.

iv   Hinkelman "A Deeper Look."

v   Hinds, Rebecca, "The 1 Trait 94 Percent of C-Suite Women Share (And How to Get It), Inc., inc.com/Rebecca-hinds/the-1-trait-94-percent-of-women-share-and-how-to-get-it.html#:~:text=the%20research%20found%20that%2094,-between%20athleticism%20and%20business%20success

vi   "Coaching Through a Gender Lens: Maximizing Girls' Play and Potential," Women's Sports Foundation, April 2019, womenssportsfoundation.org/wp-content/uploads/2019/04/coaching-through-a-gender-lens-executive-summary-web-1.pdf

vii   "Coaching Through a Gender Lens," Women's Sports Foundation.

viii   Goleman, Daniel, Emotional Intelligence: Why It Can Matter More than IQ (New York: Macmillan, 2000) pg XV

ix   "Building Blocks of Emotional Intelligence: 12 Leadership Competency Primers," Key Step Media, https://www.keystepmedia.com/shop/12-leadership-competency-primers/#.YLA6gi2cYUE

x   Bradberry, Travis, "The Massive Benefits of Boosting your Emotional Intelligence," World Economic Forum, accessed May 11, 2021, https://www.weforum.org/agenda/2020/02/emotional-intelligence-career-life-personal-development.

xi   Steenbarger, Brett, "Two Powerful Reasons to Keep a Journal,"Forbes.com, accessed May 11, 2021, https://www.forbes.com/sites/brettsteenbarger/2015/07/10/two-powerful-reasons-to-keep-a-journal/?sh=308980e2e1e2

xii   Walker, Matthew, Why We Sleep: Unlocking the Power of Sleep and Dreams (New York: Scribner, 2017) pg 215

xiii   Alex P. Linley and Stephen Joseph, eds., *Positive Psychology in Practice* (New Jersey: John Wiley and Sons Inc., 2004), pg 468-470. https://www.researchgate. net/profile/Julian-Barling/publication/232553222_Leading_Well_Transformational_Leadership_and_Well-Being/links/59f7575baca272607e2d7da9/ Leading-Well-Transformational-Leadership-and-Well-Being.pdf#page=488

xiv   Positive Psychology, Linley, pgs 44, 109

xv   Houston, Elaine, B.Sc., "How to Express Gratitude to Others: 19 Ideas + Gifts and Challenges," Positivepsychology.com, accessed May 11, 2021, https://positivepsychology.com/how-to-express-gratitude/#:~:text=1.,call%20and%20brighten%20somebody's%20day.

xvi   Passmore, J. & Marianetti, O., "The Role of Mindfulness in Coaching," The Coaching Psychologist (2007), 3(3), pg 6-7. http://www.sgcp.org.uk/publications/the-coachingpsychologist/the-role-of-mindfulness-in-coaching$.cfm

xvii   "How Often Should You Practice Mindfulness?" Pinnable Beauty, pinnablebeauty.com, xhttps://pinnablebeauty.com/how-often-should-you-practice-mindfulness/#:~:text=Answer%3A%20You%20should%20practice%20mindfulness,-time%20periods%20throughout%20the%20day.

xviii   "Coaching Through a Gender Lens: Maximizing Girls' Play and Potential," Women's Sports Foundation, pg 3 https://www.womenssportsfoundation.org/ wp-content/uploads/2019/04/coaching-through-a-gender-lens-executive-summary-web-1.pdf

xix   Bahrke, M. S., & Morgan, W. P. (1978). Anxiety reduction following exercise and meditation. Cognitive Therapy and Research, 2(4), 323–333. https://doi. org/10.1007/BF01172650

xx   "The Science of Awe," Allen, Summer Ph.D., Greater Good Science Center at UC Berkeley, for the John Templeton Foundation. Sept 2018. https://ggsc.berkeley.edu/images/uploads/GGSC-JTF_White_Paper-Awe_FINAL.pdf

xxi "The Science of Awe," Allen, Summer Ph.D. https://ggsc.berkeley.edu/images/uploads/GGSC-JTF_White_Paper-Awe_FINAL.pdf

xxii Shiota, M. N., Neufeld, S. L., Yeung, W. H., Moser, S. E., & Perea, E. F. (2011). Feeling good: Autonomic nervous system responding in five positive emotions. Emotion, 11(6), 1368–1378. https://doi.org/10.1037/a0024278

xxiii Zhang, Piff, Iyer, Koleva, & Keltner, Journal of Environmental Psychology, Published by Elsevier Ltd., Volume 37, March 2014, Pages 61-72 https://www.sciencedirect.com/science/article/abs/pii/S0272494413000893

xxiv Kaufman, Keith A., Glass, Carol R., Pineau, Timothy R., Mindful Sport Performance Enhancement: Mental Training for Athletes and Coaches (Washington D.C.: American Psychological Association, 2017)

xxv "Webinar: Emotional Agility Coaching," Institute of Coaching.org. David, Susan, https://instituteofcoaching.org/resources/webinar-emotional-agility-coaching-resource

xxvi Locke, E. A., Shaw, K. N., Saari, L. M., & Latham, G. P. (1981). Goal setting and task performance: 1969–1980. Psychological Bulletin, 90(1), 125–152. https://doi.org/10.1037/0033-2909.90.1.125

xxvii Montgomery, Kimberly J., Seeherman, Kimberly R., Haxby James V. "The Well-Tempered Social Brain." Psychological Science. Volume: 20 issue: 10, page(s): 1211-1213 Article first published online: October 1, 2009; Issue published: October 1, 2009 https://journals.sagepub.com/doi/full/10.1111/j.1467-9280.2009.02428.x

xxviii Lyubomirski, Sonja, Ph.D., The How of Happiness, a New Approach to Getting the Life You Want (New York: Penguin Books, Illustrated Edition, 2008) pg 107

xxix Goleman, Daniel, "Hot to Help," Greater Good Magazine, March 1, 2008, https://greatergood.berkeley.edu/article/item/hot_to_help

xxx   "The role of empathy and sympathy in coaching," Gloveworx blog, Nov 8, 2018, https://instituteofcoaching.org/resources/webinar-emotional-agility-coaching-resource

xxxi   Jowett, S., Cockerill, I.M., "Incompatibility in The Coach Athlete Partnership," The Psychologist, a publication of The British Psychological Society, July 2006, vol 18, pg 412-415

xxxii   Becker, Andrea J., "It's not What They Do, It's How they Do It. Athlete Experiences of Great Coaching," International Journal of Sports Science and Coaching. Volume 4, Number 1, 2009, pg. 99, https://journals.sagepub.com/doi/pdf/10.1260/1747-9541.4.1.93

xxxiii Hedstrom, Ryan, Ph.D., "Coaching Through Conflict: Effective Communication Strategies," Association for Applied Sport Psychology. https://appliedsportpsych.org/resources/resources-for-coaches/coaching-through-conflict-effective-communiation-strategies/

xxxiv   Wood, Warrick Ph.D., "The Power of Questioning in Sport Coaching: Why Sports Coaches Utilize Insightful Questions as a Teaching Method." Psychology Today. July 2, 2015. https://www.psychologytoday.com/us/blog/the-coach-athlete-relationship/201507/the-power-questioning-in-sport-coaching

xxxv   "In Team Sports, Chemistry Matters: sports analytics analysis reveals that past shared success among team members improves odds of future wins." ScienceDaily. ScienceDaily, 4 December 2018. www.sciencedaily.com/releases/2018/12/181204095355.htm

xxxvi   Dr. Brené Brown, Dare to Lead: Brave Work. Tough Conversations. Whole Hearts. (Random House, New York, 2018)

RECOMMENDED RESOURCES FOR A DEEPER DIVE

EMOTIONAL INTELLIGENCE TRAINING PROGRAMS:

A non-profit organization that empowers women and girls in sports with the leadership skills of emotional intelligence so that female athletes can thrive in sport and in life.
www.eifocus.org | info@eifocus.org

Beyond EI, www.BeyondEI.inc

TED TALKS:

Why Winning Doesn't Always Equal Success, by Valorie Kondos Field

Sleep Is Your Superpower, by Matthew Walker

The Power of Vulnerability, by Brené Brown

OTHER:

The Focused Athlete Podcast, on Apple Podcasts, Spotify, Pandora, and more. https://thefocusedathlete.buzzsprout.com

The Greater Good Science Center, www. https://greatergood.berkeley.edu

The Women's Sports Foundation, https://www.womenssportsfoundation.org

BOOKS:

Beyond Emotional Intelligence: A Guide to Accessing Your Full Potential
by S. Michele Nevarez

The Mindful College Applicant: Cultivating Emotional Intelligence for the Admissions Process, by Belinda H.Y. Chiu, Ed.D.

How Emotions are Made: The Secret Life of the Brain, by Lisa Feldman Barrett

Mindful Sport Performance Enhancement:Mental Training for Athletes and Coaches, by Keith A Kaufman, Carol R. Glass, Timothy R. Pineau

Flow: The Psychology of Optimal Experience, by Mihaly Csikszentmihalyi

The How of Happiness: A Scientific Approach to Getting the Life You Want, by Sonja Lyubomirsky

Quiet: The power of Introverts in a World that Can't Stop Talking, by Susan Cain

The Joy of Movement: How Exercise Helps Us Find Happiness, Hope, Connection, and Courage, by Kelly McGonigal, PhD.

Mindfulness for Beginners, by Jon Kabat-Zinn

Emotional Intelligence: Why it Can Matter more than IQ, by Dr. Daniel Goleman

Why We Sleep: Unlocking the Power of Sleep and Dreams, by Matthew Walker

ABOUT THE AUTHOR

Sarah Kivel is an Emotional Intelligence Consultant and Coach based in the San Francisco Bay Area. She works with executives, entrepreneurs, and leaders in healthcare from all over the world. She is a Meta Coach and a member of the faculty at GolemanEI. Sarah is a Professional Certified Coach through the International Coach Federation. She is